THE MAGNA CHARTA OF WOMAN

THE
MAGNA
CHARTA
OF WOMAN

By Jessie Penn-Lewis

BETHANY FELLOWSHIP, INC.
Minneapolis, Minnesota

The Magna Charta of Woman
By Jessie Penn-Lewis

Copyright © 1975
Bethany Fellowship, Inc.
All Rights Reserved

Library of Congress Catalog Card Number 75-28655

ISBN 0-87123-377-0

Originally published in 1919 by The Overcomer Book
Room, Bournemouth, England, under the title, *The
"Magna Charta" of Woman "According to the Scrip-
tures."* This edition newly edited from the 1948 British
edition, and published by special arrangement with The
Overcomer Book Room.

Scripture quotations in this book are taken from Great
Britain's Revised Version of 1884.

DIMENSION BOOKS
Published by Bethany Fellowship, Inc.
6820 Auto Club Road, Minneapolis, Minnesota 55438

Printed in the United States of America

O woman, that publishest good tidings to Zion, get thee up into the high mountain; O woman, that publishest good tidings to Jerusalem, lift up thy voice with strength; lift it up, be not afraid; say unto the cities of Judah, Behold your God (Isa. 40:9, lit. Hebrew).

The Lord giveth the word: The women that publish the tidings are a great host (Ps. 68:11).

Contents

About the Author

Born in 1861 in South Wales, this daughter of a mining engineer was nurtured in the "lap of Calvinistic Methodism," as she put it. Surrounded by love and a large library, she ventured into a life of learning and activity which always seemed far beyond the capability of her persistently frail body. Strong-willed and independent, she walked at the age of nine months, and by the age of four could read the Bible freely, without having been taught to read.

She married at the age of eighteen, was converted to Christ eighteen months later, and set about to learn to follow God.

At the age of thirty-one she was baptized with the Spirit, and her simple motto became, "Keep free to follow the will of God." God gave her remarkable insight into the Scriptures, and it became obvious the He had fashioned her to be a teacher.

Her ministry took her to Sweden, Russia, Finland, India, Canada and the United States. Her life became linked to the spiritual giants of her generation—F. B. Meyer, Andrew Murray, D. L. Moody.

She founded *The Overcomer*, a serious journal on the pursuit of the deeper Christian life. For many years she addressed great audiences at vast conventions of Christians. Finally, after one such series of talks she arrived home obviously ill. Her strength waned rapidly and she slipped into the presence of Christ in 1927 at the age of sixty-six.

Few women in modern times have left so profound an impression on their generation, and few have so boldly and biblically stated the value of their gender. Jessie Penn-Lewis was the embodiment of Women's Liberation in its best and noblest sense.

Introduction

"It is incumbent upon Christian women to explain themselves," writes the Editor of *The Living Way*, published in California. "They profess, as Christians, obedience to the Word of God. They think that St. Paul forbade women to speak in public, and that he discountenanced women teachers of the Bible. Yet they teach and pray and preach; and they do not even 'veil' when they do these things. . . . With [women] rests the responsibility to explain the Apostle Paul in a convincing manner, as not in opposition to their conduct. It is not enough for a woman to say 'I must leave such matters to better scholars than I; but in the meantime I will teach or preach, because I know the Spirit prompts me to do so.' [But] a woman who is called to 'preach' is likewise *called to an understanding of the Word* which will agree with that inward voice. It is the Word and the Spirit by which we must be led. . . . Perhaps in days past it was impossible for women to grasp the means of solving these problems that face the Christian women—*why the Holy Spirit should seem to move in one direction*, and the Bible point the other way, but that day has passed. Our colleges and universities are open to women. They can study Greek and Hebrew, with all essential help, as well as men. And now they should surmount these mental and spiritual perplexities. . . . They should equip themselves, as biblical scholars, to explain St. Paul as not at variance with their practice, or else they should keep silence in the churches. . . ."

The editor who writes thus exactly expresses the present situation. The hour has come when it is necessary that "Christian women should explain themselves," if the work of women in the service of Christ is not to lag behind the work of women in the world. The emancipation of women has burst upon the world as one of the epoch-making results of the Great War. It is now impossible to stay the advancing tide. The noble work of the women of the country has, it is admitted, saved the British Empire. Many men who believed that women were "called" and "fitted" only for domestic life may be said to owe their lives to the womanhood of the nation proving the falsity of their theory.

The question now is whether the *Christian* women, in their witness for Christ, are to share in this emancipation or are they to be kept back while their confrères in the world have every door opened to them. The question also goes much deeper than this. It touches the authority and infallibility of the Word of God and its divine fitness to meet the needs of every generation. It cannot be that the women of today are to be liberated for full share in the *work of the world* and at the same time have restrictions placed upon them in the *work of God*. For if this be so, all the emancipated women of the world must consent to retire to a narrower sphere of service when they become Christians, morally bound to conform their lives to the written Word of God.

In this matter the Bible itself is challenged. Is it "out of date" for the guidance of the women of today? It has consequently become imperative that Christian women themselves should now search into this question and "explain themselves" and their true status from these Scriptures, so that it may be seen that the Bible is not an antiquated Book, out of harmony with the present times. The Church of Christ *as it was originally constituted*, without the addition of centuries of man-made laws, is not out of harmony with the principles of all the successive movements of God in the world itself.

But where are the Christian women to obtain the knowledge necessary for thus independently searching the Scriptures, seeing that there are but few with the training necessary for such independent research? "The hour produces the man" is a saying which can be altered into "The hour produces the woman," to meet the woman's need of knowledge on this vital subject.

"We are acquainted with a woman," writes the editor of *The Living Way*, "who has taken the matter very seriously. Katharine Bushnell, M.D., feeling called to a public ministry, early resolved that her practice and teaching should correspond. She would not let her zeal outrun her reverence for St. Paul and his instructions. If the voice within could not be silenced in its demand that she preach and teach the Word of God, then that same voice could be relied upon to teach her how her call could be consistent with God's Word. Years of prayerful meditation over the Word, patient, persistent study of the sacred languages, and a delving in all works on Bible exposition promising any help (God placing within her reach the great libraries of England[1]), have brought an abundant reward. She has recorded some of the results of these years of research in a Bible correspondence course for women—so

1. E.g., The British Museum and the Gladstone Library at Hawarden.

that other women can 'enter into her labours,' and begin their studies where she has left off.''

Dr. Bushnell was an intimate colleague of the late Mrs. Josephine Butler, who, on the eve of her death, gave her a last charge that with her knowledge of the original languages of the Bible she would devote herself to the educating of her sex in God's teaching about women in the Scriptures. In accordance with this promise, Dr. Bushnell has for years been conducting a Bible correspondence course for women, with the lessons issued in mimeograph sheets at periodic intervals. Again and again she was urged to give forth her knowledge in print, but her reply was that the time had not yet come. But now at the psychological moment when the minds of men have been opened by the discovery of the dormant capabilities of women, she has been manifestly guided of God to issue the first series of lessons in book form, under the title of *God's Word to Women.* [2] They cover the whole ground of the status of womanhood from the beginning in the book of Genesis to the teaching of Paul in the New Testament. The lessons open up the Scriptures in a way which can only be described as containing a revelation direct from God to those who have sought to be faithfully obedient to the Spirit of God in His lead-

2. Published by the author, Oakland, CA.

ings to public service, convinced that in His own season God would bring to light the true meaning of the words of St. Paul which *appeared* to be opposed to the known mind of the Holy Spirit in their personal experience.

We gratefully recognize also that Dr. Bushnell, in doing this invaluable service to Christian women at this time, does her work with scholarly dignity and soberness of language, revealing the mind of a true scholar, whose only concern is to arrive at *truth* and not, as prejudiced persons might suppose, as a "woman" herself, endeavoring to stretch any possible point to prove her case. She also repudiates any "desire to discuss 'which is the greater in the Kingdom of Heaven, man or woman,' as an unworthy question to raise at all," and is concerned only that women, as women, should know and fulfill their destiny as ordained of God. Emphatically, too, she acknowledges the Scriptures as the infallible Word of God, with the early chapters of Genesis as true history. She says, "We are convinced that they are history, and to women very valuable history. But even if we did not believe this, women could not afford to ignore them, for the sufferings of women from a false interpretation of their teachings, have been no unreality. . . ."

Thank God, at last with the aid of this God-given light Christian women can "explain themselves," and thank God still more that the infallible Word of God is proved to be the very "Word of God" in truth by the harmony of its bedrock principles with the world movements of God in the present day. The sovereign Lord of the universe, who is bringing about the liberation of nationalities, is also emancipating womanhood from the bondage of centuries and thereby proving himself again to be the God of the Bible. He has never changed His original purpose toward the creatures He made, and never decreed, as theology, colored by Judaism, has taught, that in the dispensation of grace the largest number of His redeemed church should be relegated to a lower status than that which was given to them through the atoning work of the Son of God.

Many may say that there is no need to trouble about Paul's supposed teachings today since women in general have won their freedom and nothing can ever put them back where they were before the Great War. But, in fact, the need to explain the Apostle's language is greater, for the tide of liberation will not reach the *Christian women*, those who are born of the Spirit and seek to conform their lives to the Word of God, unless they can be shown that their liberation is in harmony with that Word. For this they must understand for themselves their true destiny as revealed in the Scriptures of truth, or else they will hold back from fulfilling the purpose of God for them in these closing days of the Age. Other women who know not God will fill the leading positions which are increasingly being opened to them on every hand.

When God's time comes to remove a veil from His Word, nothing can hinder the fulfillment of His will. He is sovereign Lord of the universe, and He has permitted for some good purpose the centuries of misrepresentation and misinterpretation of His mind concerning women, even though the "trail of the serpent" is visible all along the line. We believe it will be a cause of unspeakable thankfulness to multitudes of Christian women when they know the truth, for the dark shadow of Paul's (supposed) relegation of them to perpetual subordination on account of Eve's deception has clouded their spiritual sense of the justice of God and their apprehension of the fullness of the gospel message. Christian men, too, who have known the truth in their inner consciousness will rejoice in the light now given.

Reviewing Dr. Bushnell's book, we are bound to say it is singularly free from extravagances. Her language is restrained and dignified. Sometimes we find a little sarcasm, but knowing what she knows and having seen what she has seen of the results in the world of the Gen. 3:16 misinterpretation, nothing but the grace of God has enabled her to write so temperately.

Here and there may be some "thoughts" which might seem farfetched, but they are as legitimate an exegesis of the text as any others and do not affect any vital and fundamental New Testament doctrine. For instance, she says that she cannot find the place "where the Bible says that Eve was expelled from Eden." "Adam was thrust out with a flaming sword between him and the tree of life, lest he put forth his hand, and take of the tree of life, and eat, and live for ever" (Gen. 3:22). But since Eve was "living" spiritually, there was no such need to cut her off from the tree! "He drove out the *man*." Dr. Bushnell continues, "I choose to believe that something of the odours of Eden have enveloped Motherhood ever since creation." If deep hidden instinct is any evidence of an intuitive knowledge of some facts of life as they exist in the sight of God, Dr. Bushnell's faith is shared by men and women alike, many of whom own that there is no more beautiful reminder of Eden with its odors than the picture of a young mother with her newborn child. Dr. Bushnell suggests, too, that if Eve had heeded God's warning that she was "turning" to Adam and what the consequences would be, not yielding to this "turning," Adam might have been saved from the effects of his fall. Who is to say that this was not so? William Law declares that

Adam lost much of his perfection before Eve was formed, and she was elaborated to prevent "worse effects of his fall, and to prepare a means of his recovery."

Concerning the sending forth of this edition, I refer to some reasons for its issue from the spiritual standpoint at the close, but here I would say in connection with the original book itself that I am constrained to send out part of its message in this simple form because (1) the complete edition is so full of deep, solid information that many women who need its truths may not have the foundational knowledge for grasping at this time, and (2) the book has had to be issued at a price which is prohibitive to widespread circulation while the need for knowledge of the truths it contains is urgent.

It is my hope, therefore, that this edition will be a signpost, pointing those who desire full knowledge of the subject to the original book, *God's Word for Women,* which contains much which has not been touched upon here, such as "God's law of marriage" and other deeply vital aspects of the theme. With Dr. Bushnell's permission, I have sought to give as simply as possible the main points of some of the lessons concerning those aspects of the subject which affect the ministry of Christian women in the service of God.

Jessie Penn-Lewis, 1919

1

"Ye All Can Prophesy. . . ."

Let us consider the three passages in the New Testament which contain the teaching of Paul concerning the ministry of Christian women in the Church of Christ. As our examination of them involves questioning the rendering of the original text by translators, it would be well first to emphasize the vast debt we owe to the labors of scholars in the translation of the Scriptures and to remind ourselves of the fact that, as Schofield has said, "the labours of competent scholars have brought our English Versions to a degree of perfection so remarkable, that we may confidently rest upon them as authoritative." That this is so we gratefully admit, but, we are bound to add, with the exception of passages relating to the status of women. These most sorely need revision as must surely be acknowledged by all who honestly weigh the facts set forth by Dr. Bushnell who says, "It is very serious to base principles of action on translations of obscure passages—those upon which no translators can dogmatise."

But "it is not worth our while," writes Dr. Bushnell, "to complain that men have not always seen truths that had no special application to their needs, either in interpreting or in translating the Bible; we merely wish to point out wherein there is need of changes. . . . Supposing women only had translated the Bible from age to age, is there a likelihood that men would have rested content with the outcome? Therefore our brothers have no good reason to complain if, while conceding that men have done the best they could, alone, we assert that they did not do the best that could have been done. The work would have been of a much higher order had they first helped women to learn the sacred languages . . . and then have given them a place on the translation committees. . . ."

For "there are truths," Dr. Bushnell rightly says, "that give light upon problems that women alone are called upon to solve," and "such truths man is not equipped to understand, much less to set forth to the understanding of women."

Canon Payne Smith says of the Bible, "A bad translation of this Book exercises a depressing influence upon a nation's civilisation; a good translation is one of the great levers in a nation's rise." This is especially so in the effect of a "bad translation" connected with the status of women in general. For, as Dr. Bushnell observes, the reason why "so large a proportion of the women of Christendom are given over to fashion and folly" is that they have never been "given a proper and dignified work in the advancement of God's kingdom. . . ." And this because three passages in the epistles of Paul have been rendered into English in such a way that they have entirely misinterpreted the teaching of the Apostle, and by so doing have shut out women from "proper and dignified work" in the church of God.

Now let us turn to 1 Cor. 14:34, 35 and see what fresh light Dr. Bushnell brings to bear upon it. It reads in the R.V. thus:

> Let the women keep silence in the churches: for it is not permitted unto them to speak: but let them be in subjection, as also saith the law. And if they would learn anything, let them ask their own husbands at home: for it is shameful for a woman to speak in the church.

By minute examination of the original Greek text, references to authoritative scholars and the historical setting of the occasion calling forth the epistle, Dr. Bushnell shows clearly that Paul never wrote these words as a "commandment of the Lord," but was *quoting what the Judaizers*

in the Corinthian church were saying. Their mis-
chief making at Corinth was in connection with
the work of Christian women as in other ways.
This simplifies the entire subject, if the statement
proves to be in harmony with the context and
other parts of scripture.

Referring to the various attempts which have
been made to reconcile Paul's words about women
praying and prophesying (I Cor. 11:5: "But every
woman praying or prophesying with her head unveiled dishonoureth her head. . ."") with his seem-
ing command, "Let the women keep silence," in
1 Cor. 14:34, Dr. Bushnell points out some weak
points in the explanations and expresses what
many Christian women have felt, that most of
these attempts have not solved the difficulty sat-
isfactorily. "The Holy Spirit does not descend to
sophistry to induce women to do the will of God,"
says Dr. Bushnell. Nor does Paul, as Prof. Ramsay suggests, use "tortuous special pleading,"
or resort to "Jewish fables" to "find a pretext
for silencing women." For Paul spoke as "the
mouthpiece of God," and his writings were
prompted by the Holy Spirit. Therefore a "consistent worthy sense can be found" in his words,
if his arguments are not twisted out of conformity
with Scriptures. For it is a safe rule that scripture must interpret scripture under the illumina-
tion of the Spirit of God, and when it does so,

it will be found to have no contradictions. The
true interpretation carries with it, to a spiritual
mind, a reasonableness and simplicity which is
worthy of God.

So it appears in this instance. That Paul is
but quoting the language of the Judaizers in
1 Cor. 14:34, 35 is in harmony with previous parts
of the epistle. Again and again from chapter 5
on to end of chapter 14, it can be seen that he
is replying to a letter of questions sent to him
by the Corinthian Church. In instance after instance it can be detected that "the reference to
the questions is repeated whenever a new point
is taken up."[1]

We need to remember that in the Greek manu-
scripts there were no capital letters to words,
no quotation marks, and no punctuation such as
we have in our English versions of the Bible.
So those who use a translation (e.g., English) are
dependent upon the translators for the addition
of these valuable and necessary aids in obtaining
the sense of the original. From the Greek text
itself there is no means of knowing when a sentence is a quotation or when it expresses the mind
of the writer except by internal and contextual
evidences and careful examination of the historical setting of the words. Even then "few are the

1. Conybeare and Howson's translation of the epistle brings
out clearly many of these "quotations."

translators, fewer the exegetes ... to abstain from finding in the Bible thoughts which it does not contain, and rejecting, or unjustly modifying, the thoughts which are indeed there," says Archdeacon Farrar.

How solemn, then, the fact that for centuries Christian women have been robbed of their true status in the Church of Christ because translators, and many expositors, have failed to perceive the true setting of the Apostle's words. But God is giving the true light on this subject at the time when it is most needed for women's service in the world. Scholars are now in possession of greatly increased knowledge of facts connected with early church history and other subjects which enables them to understand better the writings of the New Testament. Some appear to be beginning to see that the key of "quotations" from the letter of the Corinthian Church to Paul unlocks some problems as to the meaning of some statements in his epistles, statements which have hitherto been beyond solution. For example, Professor Sir William Ramsay, the most widely accepted authority on St. Paul in the present day and known for his researches in the history of the early church in Asia Minor, "an extensive writer about St. Paul, his epistles, and journeys," says: "*We should be ready to suspect Paul is making a quotation* from the letter addressed to him by the Corinthians, whenever he alludes to their knowledge, or when any statement *stands in marked contrast* either with the immediate context, or with Paul's known views."

Dr. Bushnell observes that this "marked contrast" is obvious when 1 Cor. 14:34, 35 is placed alongside of 1 Cor. 11:5, for Paul must have written the words in chapter 14 not more than half an hour after the previous ones, which show clearly that women were accustomed both to pray and to preach in public. Moreover, that 1 Cor. 14:34, 35 contained a "quotation" of the Judaizers' words is confirmed when it is considered in detail. "*It is not permitted,*" says someone, for women "*to speak . . . as also saith the law . . .*" (v. 34). But this cannot refer to the Old Testament Scriptures, for there is not one trace, from Genesis to Malachi, of any such prohibition, nor is there a single word in the whole "law of Moses" dealing with the subject. [2]

Therefore the words "*it is not permitted*" and "*as also saith the law*" must refer to some "rule" outside of Scripture. There was no other but the Oral Law of the Jews, appealed to by the Judaizers in the church in their efforts at that time to bring Christianity back within the confines of Judaism. That the words "as saith

---

2. That it did not refer to "Gen. 3:16" as "the law" will be seen on reading chapter 6, p. 85.

the law" referred to the Oral Law of the Jews is recognized by some scholars, for a well-known lexicographer, in his Greek-Latin Lexicon, says that "as saith the law" refers to the Jewish Oral Law, which did teach the silencing of women. The Talmud also taught that it was "a shame for a woman to let her voice be heard among men"—almost the very words used in the language quoted by the Apostle.

Again, the reference to the "law" is, of itself, sufficient to show that the Apostle, who labored so earnestly to free the Christian Church from the very shadow of Judaism, as his epistles show, was not expressing his own conviction in the language attributed to him. Paul never appealed to the "law" for the guidance of the Church of Christ, but, on the contrary, declared that believers were "*dead to the law* by the body of Christ" (Rom. 7:4), that they might serve in newness of spirit and not the oldness of the letter (v. 6). Then how could he say consistently, "Let the women keep silence . . . *as also saith the law*," even were such a prohibition to be found in the law of Moses?

It is therefore clear that the Apostle was quoting what the Judaizers in the Corinthian Church were saying. For, as Dr. Bushnell writes, "many were in it as 'false brethren' to destroy it (2 Cor. 10:12; Gal. 2:4) . . . and others were honestly, but mistakenly, working to the same end, but with better motives. . . . None of them could hope to influence the Christians to return to . . . the traditions of the Jews by attacking things that were regular. . . . The only opportunity lay in something irregular, and this they found in the public prophesying of women. The Oral Law had said 'It is a shame,' and the Judaizers took up the cry that 'the women must keep silence' . . . 'they must ask their husbands at home.' . . . 'It is a shame for a woman to speak in the assembly, the Oral Law of the Jews says so,' etc. All this was written to Paul from Corinth. He copies it out for his text. He shows up its sophistries, [and] exhorts his converts to be jealous of their gift of prophecy in the church. . . ."

As to the women "asking questions of their husbands at home," Dr. Bushnell points out that it is not known that even men asked questions in church as the Jews did in the synagogue. If Paul said these words as a command, in the condition of the Corinthian and other churches of that time, he would be sending some women back to heathenism or Judaism for spiritual help or, in some cases, to no "help" at all, since many might be without husbands.

Let us look now at the context of 1 Cor. 14: 34, 35, and see how the "quotation" fits into its place as a quotation. To grasp the subject clearly

it would be well to read chapters 12, 13, and 14
in the R.V., remembering that in the original
Greek manuscript there were no chapter divisions or texts to split up the matter into verses.
The theme from the beginning of chapter 12 is
one coherent whole, and verses 4-11 of that chapter
form the basis and key to all that is afterward
written.

Paul is dealing with the subject of the mystical
Body of Christ and the operations of God the Holy
Spirit in and through the *living members of the
Body*. In verses 12-30 he describes the Body itself,
the mystical church, and the way in which each
member is joined up and set in his place by God
the Spirit (vv. 18-28). Then comes the picture of
the love life of God to be shown forth in each
member (ch. 13), followed by a very full opening up of the subject of "preaching," or as it
was termed by Paul, "prophesying," in chapter 15. The believers were to "follow after love"
as the first essential, and desire all spiritual
"gifts." But the primary gift was prophecy—
power to declare God's message either by the
prophetic gift or speaking to edification, and
"exhortation and comfort." This was a necessity
for the growth of God's children (vv. 3, 12, 19),
as well as for the conviction of those "without"
the church (vv. 24, 25). Then in verse 26 the
Apostle pictures a gathering of the members of

the local church—the assembly which in Corinth was probably held in the house of Gaius (1 Cor. 1:14; Rom. 16:23). He pictures one and another present. "What is it then, brethren?" he writes. Here we must remember, as Dr. Bushnell points out, "that the word 'brethren' was more like 'sisters' in Greek than in English." The difference is only between "*adelphos* (brother) and *adelphē* (sister)." Moreover, "masculine and feminine nouns and adjectives very generally had the same form in New Testament Greek." In English "it is only by an effort of thought that women take the word 'brethren' to themselves, but not so the Greek *adelphoi.* . . ."

"What is it then, brethren? When ye come together, each one hath a psalm, hath a teaching, hath a revelation." This would easily produce confusion, and so the Apostle directs that each one may speak "by course" but all "unto edifying." "For," he writes, "ye all can prophesy one by one, that *all* may learn, and *all* may be exhorted" (v. 31, R.V.m.). "God is not a God of confusion, but of peace; as in all the churches[3] of the saints" (v. 33).

"All" might prophesy, said the Apostle, that "*all* may learn," as God gave the word of wisdom

---

3. "Ecclesia," assembly or congregation, meaning simply the local gatherings of believers, established in the first centuries of Christianity.

or word of knowledge to one and the other—
surely women as well as men—both "alls" obviously including *all* who might be in the assembly. This was Paul's light from God for the
church at Corinth, in answer to the objections
of the Judaizers, which he now proceeds to quote.
The very writing of the words seems to stir his
indignation, for he follows them with the abrupt
exclamation or question "What? was it from *you*
[Judaizers, or criticizers, at Corinth] that the
word of God went forth? or came it unto you
alone? . . . If any man thinketh himself to be
spiritual [see ch. 12:1—*knowing the Spirit, and
what comes from Him*], let him take knowledge
of the things which I write unto you, that they
are the *commandment of the Lord*" (vv. 36, 37).

In reference to the expression "the word of
God," Dr. Bushnell points out that it has a
definite and specific sense in the New Testament,
"as referring either to the Gospel or prophetic ut-
terance given from above."[4] In this again scripture interprets scripture. Paul is referring to the
word of God in its *coming forth from God* and
its *going forth through* His messengers. He has
been explaining how the Spirit of God gave to
one and the other in the Body of Christ "the
Word" and the gift of prophecy. Could the Judai-

4. See Luke 3:1, 2, 5; Rom. 9:6; 1 Thess. 1:8, 2:13; 2 Cor.
2: 17, 4:2.

zers claim that it had come to them alone and
gone forth out of them and no others? Were they
the final authority as to who should speak when
God gave the message? If any man among the
objectors was "spiritual," it would be evidenced
by his recognizing that *all* the things that Paul
had written were "*the commandment of the
Lord,*" notwithstanding the "precepts of men" in
the Oral Law of the Jews.

"Paul's contention is," writes Dr. Bushnell,
that "since the Spirit of prophecy . . . did not . . .
come forth from anyone but God, to attempt to
control 'prophecy' by restrictions as to who may
utter it means a dictating to God as to what
instruments He may employ."

That Paul was quoting the Judaizers in the
language he used in these verses again is made
still more evident when we consider the historical
setting, which may be briefly summarized as follows.

The Corinthian Church had written Paul a
letter and he is answering it. There were divisions
among them. He had enemies at Corinth who dis-
puted his right to be called an apostle and criti-
cized him and his companions for having a
woman traveling with them. The fact stated in
Acts 18:18 that Priscilla with Aquila her husband had left Corinth in company with Paul short-
ly before seems to make clear that the woman

referred to was Priscilla.[5] She was well known to all the churches of the Gentiles (Rom. 16:3, 4), and it is probable that Paul was writing his reply to the letter in her home at Ephesus (1 Cor. 16:19).

Now why should there be any trouble over Priscilla? It seems that Aquila was a Jew from Asia Minor and his wife was probably also a native. Here women were held in great honor. "The honours and influence which belonged to women in the cities of Asia Minor," writes Prof. Ramsay, "form one of the most remarkable features in the history of the country. . . . Under the Roman Empire we find women who are magistrates and presidents of games, who are loaded with honours. The custom of the country influenced even the Jews, who . . . in one case, appointed a woman at Smyrna to the position of ruler of the Synagogue." Out of this atmosphere of dignity and honor, Priscilla goes to Corinth expecting to take her usual position of equality with her husband! So we have the occasion for the criticism of the Judaizers and the questions of the church at Corinth!

How the early believers understood Paul's re-

---

5. The R.V. margin reads "a wife that is a sister." This could mean Paul's own wife or Priscilla, who was Aquila's wife, or the Apostle was speaking in the abstract of the principle of liberty of action.

ply to their questions on the subject is also seen in Acts 21:9, referring to Philip's "four daughters . . . which did prophesy." Dr. Bushnell observes that "not even a year after [the] Corinthian epistle was written were women yet silenced."

It all is so clear now that we know! And we cannot but marvel why this simple and obvious explanation of the words of Paul did not occur to the translators of our English versions. But we shall see the reason for their eyes being holden and their minds being closed as we turn to the other passages bearing upon this subject.

Before doing so, let us note that not *all* expositors have been blinded. Dr. Adam Clarke writes concerning 1 Cor. 14:34, 35 that it is "the *only one* in the whole Book of God which even by a false translation can be made prohibitory of female speaking in the Church. How comes it then, that by this one isolated passage, which according to our best Greek authorities, is *wrongly rendered and wrongly applied*, woman's lips have been sealed for centuries, and the 'testimony of Jesus, which is the spirit of prophecy' silenced, when bestowed on her? How is it, that this solitary text has been allowed to stand unexamined and unexplained, nay, that learned commentators who have *known* its true meaning, as perfectly as either Robinson, Bloomfield, Greenfield, Scott, Parkhurst, or Locke, *have upheld the delu-*

sion, and enforced it as a Divine precept binding on all female disciples through all time? Surely there must have been some unfaithfulness, 'craftiness,' and 'handling the word of life deceitfully' somewhere. Surely the love of caste and unscriptural jealousy for a separated priesthood has had something to do with this anomaly. By this course, divines and commentators have involved themselves in all sorts of inconsistencies and contradictions; and worse, they have nullified some of the most precious promises of God's Word. They have set the most explicit predictions of prophecy at variance with apostolic injunctions, and the most immediate and wonderful operations of the Holy Ghost, in direct opposition 'to [supposed] positive, explicit, and universal rules.' "

"Authority Over Her Head. . ."

Let us look at 1 Cor. 11:2-16 and endeavor to
understand the circumstances which occasioned
the writing of this particular passage. Otherwise,
even in the R.V. English, it conveys no intelligible
meaning to the ordinary reader. Although, as Dr.
Bushnell says, "we should not thoughtlessly as-
sume that the Bible is to be read in the light
of profane history, and corrected by it; nevertheless, when [it is] tested by well-known ancient
customs, or conditions set forth in reliable profane history, it will be found to ring true to con-
temporary facts."

The subject of the wearing of the veil is not
of great importance to Christian women today
in Western lands, except that a true understanding
of Paul's words would show that he was always
consistent in word and practice. Also, every por-

tion of the Scriptures, being inspired and given for our learning, contains some deep and eternal principle applicable to every age.

It is necessary for elucidation to deal with this passage verse by verse. We find at the beginning one of Paul's many "quotations" from the Corinthian letter. "Now I praise you," wrote the Apostle, "that *ye remember me in all things, and hold fast the traditions even as I delivered them to you*." According to Conybeare and Howson this is what the church at Corinth had said in their letter as they asked for some light on the question of the wearing of the Jewish Tallith, or veil, in worship in the Christian Church.

The real purpose of this passage, says Dr. Lightfoot, was to stop the practice of Jewish Christian men veiling in worship, according to the custom of the Jews. It seems that the Jew veiled as "a sign of reverence before God, and of condemnation for sin." The veil was called a "tallith." The Romans also veiled in worship, and the Corinthian Church consisted largely of Roman converts. Then the question arose at Corinth whether the *Christian women* as well as the Christian men should veil.

This question the Apostle now proceeds to deal with in his usual way of analogy and spiritual logic, seizing the occasion for teaching the believers at Corinth how to arrive at a "sound judg-

2

ment" for themselves in the practicable application of spiritual principles to the facts of life.

Verse 3: "*I would have you know, that the head of every man is Christ.*" Chrysostom says, "He cannot be the Head of those who are not in the Body . . . so when Paul says 'every man' one must understand it of *believers.*" It is also important to know that the Greek word used *throughout the entire passage* for "man" is *aner*—the adult male or husband, for according to the Oral Law of the Jews the married man alone was obliged to wear the tallith. "And *the head of the woman is the man*"—obviously, the head of the *wife* is the husband. "*And the head of Christ is God.*"

Verse 4: "*Every* [Christian] *man praying or prophesying, having his head covered, dishonoureth his head.*" Since the tallith was a sign of guilt and condemnation, when a *Christian* covered his head with it, a sign of condemnation, he dishonored his Head, Christ, who had atoned for all his sins. "There is . . . now no condemnation to them that are in Christ Jesus" (Rom. 8:1).

Verses 5 and 6: "*But every woman* [i.e., *wife,* since he who wore the tallith was a husband], *praying or prophesying with her head unveiled dishonoureth her* [matrimonial] *head: for it is one and the same thing as if she were shaven. 'For if a woman is not veiled, let her also be shorn': but if it is a shame to a woman to be shorn or shaven, let her be veiled."*

Here we have the fact recognized without any condemnatory comment by the Apostle that women did pray and prophesy in the church. But why the reference to "veiling," and the dishonor to her husband as her "head"? Here again the customs and the Oral Law of the Jews elucidate Paul's language, together with the clue of "quotation," for Dr. Lightfoot says that in the words, *"For if a woman is not veiled, let her also be shorn,"* Paul "does not here speak in his own sense, but cites something usual among the Jews." And it is a fact that the Oral Law decreed that if a Jewess did not cover her head, she should be "shorn"—the very greatest "shame" that was possible to a Jewish woman—so much so that a Jew might divorce his wife if she was seen abroad with her head uncovered, and "a Jew favourably disposed towards his wife's profession of Christianity, and towards the practice of unveiling in worship, might be compelled by his relatives, or the Synagogue authorities . . . to divorce his wife if she unveiled."

In the light of these circumstances, therefore, the reasoning of Paul in verses 5 and 6 is simple if read with the analogy of verse 4 in mind. The Apostle reasons that if a man dishonored his "head," Christ, by wearing the tallith when he prayed or prophesied—a veil being a sign of guilt or condemnation—so a "wife" who took part in the assembly with her head uncovered, might or would, according to the Oral Law of the Jews, bring dishonor upon her (matrimonial) "head." Therefore if unveiling her head in the church meant these consequences—shame as if she was shorn and all that it signified—then "let her be veiled"; she was not commanded to unveil like her husband.

Verse 7: *"For a* [Christian] *man indeed ought not to have his head veiled, forasmuch as he is the image and glory of God: but the woman is the glory of the man."* That the *Christian* man is referred to in the entire passage should be remembered as we read these words, for, as Dr. Bushnell remarks, "poor fallen sinful man does not bear God's image and likeness simply because he is a male. It is the glorified Jesus Christ who bears that image and manifests that glory. It is only *in Him* that humanity takes that standing before God." The analogy again is simple. A *Christian* man ought not to veil his head with a sign of condemnation, for as a *Christian* he is "the image and glory of God," and should manifest the glory of his Head in heaven. The "wife" also is the "glory" of her (matrimonial) head, and should likewise reflect honor and not dishonor upon him.

Verses 8, 9 and 10: *"For the man is not of the woman; but the woman of the man: for neither was the man created for the woman; but the woman for the man: for this cause ought the woman to have authority over her head, because of the angels. . . ."* (R.V.m.).

The 10th verse, Dean Stanley says, "in the difficulty of its several parts, stands alone in the New Testament." "But," Dr. Bushnell remarks, "the only difficulty is to make Paul say the precise opposite to what he clearly says here!" Her rendering of verses 8, 9, 10 makes them very simple. It runs as follows:

> For man is not originally from woman [as a despised and inferior source], but woman is from man. Nor was the man created for the woman, [to help her], but the woman for the man, [to help him]. For this [additional] cause ought the woman to have the authority over her head [to unveil it], because of her angels who always behold God's face.

The 10th verse, read in this way, consistently gives a logical climax to the Apostle's reasonings in the preceding verses, and the R.V. and its marginal note is very near Dr. Bushnell's reading when it says, "For this cause ought the woman to have authority over her head, because of the angels." The words "a sign of" in the text of the R.V. are in italics, indicating that they are not in the original Greek but are supplied by the translators.

The R.V. rendering, therefore, correctly does away with the fiction of "veil" as a "sign" of another's authority. Yet the A.V. (1611), and even a recent edition of the A.V. issued with the express purpose of helping students in the understanding of the Scriptures, has a note in the margin saying that "power on her head" means "*the sign* of her husband's authority." How difficult it is for fixed ideas to be removed from the minds of men, even when there are indisputable and authoritative statements to the contrary! How the idea that "power" meant a "veil" came into the teaching on 1 Cor. 11:10 is traced back historically by Dr. Bushnell to Valentinus the Gnostic and the rites of the gnostic initiation ceremonies, showing that the very first corruption of St. Paul's meaning came from this objectionable source.

But what about these angels in verse 10? The suggestions made in connection with this phrase are truly childish and unseemly, contrary to an understanding of what the atoning work of Christ has accomplished for redeemed men and women. Some expositors suggest some peril from the spirit world which demands a veil as protection for the praying woman, so that even in private prayer she is to be covered; whereas the only protection from the interference of evil spirits with man or woman engaged in prayer is reliance upon the atoning blood of the Lamb. From the highest spiritual standpoint, which was Paul's normal condition of mind, the words mean that the woman should have unveiled access to God, as well as to her husband and the angels. This the text itself confirms in the original.

The definite article in Greek, says Dr. Bushnell, often has the force of a possessive pronoun. The words in verse 10 thus will bear the translation "because of *their* angels." This could be taken in two ways. First, in the light of Christ's word in Matt. 18:10, where He says of the "little ones" who believe in Him that "their angels do always behold the face of my Father which is in heaven," meaning that the ministering spirits called "angels," who are given charge over all believers (cf. Heb. 1:14), have always unveiled access to God, and therefore those they minister to should have unveiled access also, being in higher rank (in Christ) than the angels who minister to them. Or the word "angels" may be used by Paul to denote what an old mystical writer, William Bromley, wrote a hundred years ago, that the spirit of the believer is called his "angel," "because it stands between God and our outward man, receiving directions from Him for [its] rule and government."

Verses 11, 12 and 13: "*Nevertheless, neither is the woman without the man, nor the man with-*

*out the woman, in the Lord. For as the woman
is of the man, so is the man also by the woman;
but all things are of God. Judge ye in yourselves:
is it seemly that a woman pray unto God unveiled?"*

These verses contain Paul's reminder of the
oneness in Christ of men and women "in the
Lord." He had been obliged to refer to each apart
from the other, but the true spiritual position of
both was one in Christ, neither able to do without
the other in the economy of grace or in the world
of men. So his final word is that, having reasoned
the matter out for those he was writing to, they
were now able to come to a conclusion and "judge
among themselves," and decide, "is it seemly that
a woman pray unto God unveiled" (v. 13). The
removal of the interrogation mark placed to these
words makes all the difference, and the removal
is legitimate because, as Dr. Bushnell points out,
there is no interrogative word in the sentence
in the original Greek, nor does the Greek "alter
the order of the words of a sentence to distinguish
a question from a simple statement as we do in
English." *The interrogation mark alone changes
the statement into a question in the English version.*

Verses 14 and 15: *"Doth not even nature itself
teach you, that, if a man have long hair, it is*

a dishonour to him? But if a woman have long hair, it is a glory to her: for her hair is given her for a covering."

A simple statement in these verses has again been turned into a question by the punctuation added "centuries later than when St. Paul wrote these words." The Apostle thus appears to make statements that are obviously contrary to the facts of nature and of history. For, as Dr. Bushnell says, "nature" does not teach that if a man has "long hair" it is "a dishonour" to him—millions of men in China wear long hair, and "nature has never taught them that it is a shame." Furthermore, the Corinthians to whom Paul was writing boasted that they were "descendants of the long-haried Achaeans, celebrated in the Greek poem, Homer's Iliad." It would therefore be a most strange question for Paul to put to them, while to Jews long hair in fulfillment of religious vows (Num. 6:1-21) was a glory, not a shame.

But why does Paul refer to hair at all? Again we need to understand Jewish customs. Perpetually Paul had to be countering not only the customs but the influence of Judaistic thought upon Christians only gradually emerging into apprehension of the full liberty of the gospel. The Apostle had just said that a woman should have "authority over her own head" to veil or unveil as she judged best. But the Oral Law had made unveiling so disgraceful a thing that Christian women would find it difficult to put away the veil, even when circumstances were favorable to doing so. The Apostle then meets this difficulty by saying that the woman already had a veil that was a glory to her—her own hair—and so she need not be ashamed of uncovering it, whatever the Judaizers might say.

Verse 16: *"But if any man seemeth to be contentious, we have no such custom, neither the churches of God."*

Here is the conclusion of the passage, and it should be read in the light of all that has preceded it. In effect Paul says: If the women under specially difficult circumstances wish to veil, they are to have "authority over their head" to do so or not, as they please. But "if any man seemeth to be contentious" about it, let him know that as Christians and as a church we "have no such custom" of veiling.

The summing up of the whole passage is given as follows by Dr. Bushnell. "Paul (1) forbids men to veil (since there is now no condemnation to them which are in Christ Jesus); (2) permits women to veil; but (3) guards against this permission being construed as a command by showing that ideally the woman should unveil before God, man and angels; (4) shows that there is special propriety in women unveiling when addressing God in prayer; (5) declares that (contrary to the teaching of the Jews) there is nothing for a woman to be ashamed of in showing her hair, for it is a 'glory' to her; and (6) disavows veiling as a church custom." In confirmation of the correctness of this interpretation of the whole passage, Dr. Bushnell remarks that a "little historical evidence . . . ought to go a long way" in proving that the Apostle did not forbid women unveiling, for it is an undisputed fact in church history (see Dean Alford in comments on 1 Tim. 5:9) that "women sat unveiled in the assemblies in a separate place, by the presbyters," and were "ordained by the laying on of hands" until the Church Council of Laodicea forbade it in 363 A.D.—three hundred years after Paul had written the Epistle to the Corinthians.

Dr. Bushnell has much more to say than this on the subject, for she devotes two further lessons to tracing back through church history how the misinterpretation of Paul's true teaching on the veil came into and colored the later versions of the English Bible.

3

"Thoroughly Deceived . . . but . . . !"

The third obscure passage in Paul's writings upon which the misinterpretation of Paul's teaching about women is based is 1 Tim. 2:8-15, written *ten years later* than the first Epistle to the Corinthians. It reads as follows in the R.V.:

> I desire therefore that the men pray in every place, lifting up holy hands, without wrath and disputing. In like manner, that women adorn themselves in modest apparel, with shamefastness and sobriety; not with braided hair, and gold or pearls or costly raiment; but (which becometh women professing godliness) through good works. Let a woman learn in quietness with all subjection. But I permit not a woman to teach, nor to have dominion[1] over a man, but to be in quietness. For Adam was first formed, then Eve; and Adam was not beguiled, but the woman being be-

---

1. The word "usurp" (A.V.) is not in the original.

> guiled hath fallen into transgression: but she shall
> be saved through the childbearing, if they con-
> tinue in faith and love and sanctification with
> sobriety.

Here again let us remember that there are no punctuation marks in the Greek; and here, too, the historical setting of the words is of very great importance. For apart from historical light upon the circumstances calling forth the language used by the Apostle, it is difficult to get a clear understanding of what he means.

When Paul was arrested and taken to Caesarea for trial, he there appealed unto Caesar and was sent to Rome, where he arrived in A.D. 31, in the seventh year of Nero's reign. He was after-wards allowed to dwell in his own hired house and in time gathered a "church" or "assembly" (Gr.) about him. Paul was well known throughout the Praetorian guard of Nero as a prisoner for Christ, and he sends greeting to the Philippian Church from the Christians in the Imperial house-hold of Nero.

The moral state of things which surrounded Paul in Rome at this time can be realized only by reading the history of that period. Nero was "the most infamous potentate that ever disgraced a throne." Tacitus, a pagan historian, writes that "he punished with exquisite torture [the] Christians. . . . Some were covered with skins of wild beasts, and left to be devoured by dogs; others were nailed to the cross, numbers were burnt alive; and many covered over with inflammable matter were lighted up . . . as torches during the night. . . ." All Christians, women and men, were therefore in the greatest peril. Paul was probably in Spain when he heard of the awful martyrdom of the Roman Church in A.D. 64, and it is thought that during a second imprisonment at Rome, and three years after this martyrdom of the Christians, he wrote his first epistle to Timothy in A.D. 67.

The Roman Christian Church not only had to contend with persecution by the imperial authorities, but the opposition of the Jews increased the dangers of the situation. For it seems that the Jews were in favor in Rome at this time because the emperor had married the Jewish proselyte Poppaea, while Christians were in greatest peril. Professor Ramsay says: "If the Jews appeared to the Empire to resemble the Christians so much, and yet were treated so differently, the reason . . . must have lain in those points in which Christians differed from the Jews." And Dr. Bushnell remarks, "At no point was the contrast greater at this time than in the Christian treatment of women." "For," she continues, "there were four points at any rate in which this difference was manifest: (1) in the *aggressiveness of Chris-*

tianity, whilst Judaism was proud, exclusive and unexpansive; (2) in the *instruction of women* as expressly permitted by Paul, whereas the Jewish Oral Law taught that women were only to be instructed in their own special duties . . . (3) in the many *conversions of women:* and (4) in their activity in the Apostolic Church." Lecky, in his *History of European Morals*, refers to "the very conspicuous position that female influence assumed in the great work of the conversion of the Roman Empire. In no other movement of thought was it so powerful or so acknowledged. In the ages of persecution female figures occupy many of the foremost places in the ranks of martyrdom, and pagan and Christian writers alike attest the alacrity with which women flocked to the church."

Therefore, writes Dr. Bushnell, "this aggressiveness of Christianity, and activity of Christian women, would not only offend Jews, but the complaint against it, on the part of the Jews, would make a deep impression in time upon the . . . Imperial Government. . . . Every new convert would mean fresh danger for the Church, and the aggravation would be doubled if that convert were the wife of an unbelieving husband, or the daughter of an unbelieving father." Lecky says, too, "another cause of the peculiar animosity felt against the Christians was the constant interference with domestic life, arising from the great number of female conversions. . . ."

It is necessary therefore to bear all this in mind if Paul's words to Timothy concerning the position of women in the church are to be understood. Prof. Sir. W. Ramsay points this out also when he says, "The advice given by St. Paul as to the relations of the Christians to the society in which they are placed, *is always in accordance with the situation . . . occupied by them under Nero."*

Now let us read again the passage in 1 Tim. 2:8-15, R.V., and note some points about it, taking them verse by verse.

Verse 8: *"I desire therefore that the men pray in every place, lifting up holy hands, without wrath and disputing."* This is quite clear, but now we find a full stop after the word "disputing," and then the English version (R.V.) goes on to say—

Verse 9: *"In like manner, that women adorn themselves,"* etc. But how can women *"in like manner"* adorn themselves like men? (v. 8). Conybeare and Howson say that "after the word 'women' we must supply 'pray' (as Chrysostom does)," and Prof. Ramsay says, "The necessary and inevitable sense of this word [likewise] is *that the whole body of women is to be understood as affected by what has been said about men."* In other words, that Paul wishes the women to pray "in every place" as well as the men.

Then follow suitable directions as to how the Christian women should dress, obviously when engaged in public prayer. "In times of peril," Dr. Bushnell observes, it was very reasonable "to advise the most quiet and unobtrusive dress." The deportment of women, again obviously when engaged in public service, is then referred to, but one of the words used by the Apostle is not rendered correctly, either in the A.V. or the R.V. The word in the Greek is to be found again only in Heb. 12:28, in connection with service well pleasing to God; and then it is translated "reverence" or "godly fear" (m.). A question which Christian women might well ask the translators is why they should render this particular Greek word as "shamefacedness" (A.V.) and "shamefastness" (R.V., an obsolete English word) when used in reference to women, and "reverence" or "godly fear" when it refers to the service of all believers to a God who is "consuming fire."

Verse 10: "*But (which becometh women professing godliness) through good works.*" Here, hidden away in the original text, is the very confirmation of women's public work, if Christian women had but known it! Dr. Bushnell says the word "professing" in the original "is derived from two Greek words, the preposition meaning 'upon,' or 'unto,' and [a verb] meaning '*I deliver a mes-*

sage.' The verb is the word from which we get 'angel,' which means a 'messenger.'" The word is also frequently used "in the sense of 'to promise,'" and it often means "to profess to teach." The only other passage in the New Testament where this word [in 1 Tim. 2:10] is translated "profess" is in the same Epistle in chapter 6:21, where Paul says "which some *professing* have erred concerning the faith." On the word in 1 Tim. 6:21, Professor Ramsay says, it *"regularly implies* that the person mentioned came before the public, with promises, in order to gain supporters; it is applied to candidates for . . . votes in the Greek cities, who publicly announced what they intended to do . . . if they gained popular support. . . ."

"If this be the meaning 'regularly implied' by this word," observes Dr. Bushnell, "then why not here where it relates to women? These women 'came before the public to gain supporters,' not for themselves, but to win people to the standard of the Cross, and they promise 'godliness' in place of a sin burdened life to those who will accept their offers."

But Paul has something to say quite distinctively about the woman *learner* in the next verses.

Verses 11 and 12: "*Let a woman learn in quietness with all subjection. But I permit not a woman to teach, nor to have dominion over a man, but to be in quietness."* Here let us remember Prof. Ramsay's words that Paul's advice *"is always in accordance"* with the situation of the Christians under Nero. Read in the light of verses 8-10, with their recognition of woman's public work both in prayer and preaching—*"pray* everywhere," *"proclaiming* godliness"—it is obvious, observes Dr. Bushnell, that verses 11 and 12 embody an "exceptional prudential measure to meet a dire necessity of perilous times," and are not contradictory to what the Apostle had just said.

The times were indeed perilous for Christian women. The Jews were bitterly against the teaching of women and angered by the different attitude of Christianity towards them. They might complain to the authorities and bring grave danger upon the whole body of believers. So, writes Dr. Bushnell, the Apostle tells Timothy that "a woman who comes asking to be taught" is "to be allowed to learn, but in quietness" (not "silence" as in A.V.), because of the possible persecution, and such "learners" should be willing to learn "in all subjection." [2] Also, Paul adds, that (on account of the Neronian peril) he himself did not allow a woman to do the "teaching" at such a time or to "have dominion over a man"—quite a different matter from "praying" and "pro-

---

2. See meaning of this word on page 75.

claiming" the gospel. Neither was it a permanent prohibition of "teaching" for all time as Dr. Bushnell illustrates in the following way:

"Supposing during the Armenian atrocities, or the Chinese Boxer uprising, because of some special peril to men, to which women were not exposed, a bishop had sent the following advice: 'Let male preachers of the Gospel refrain from teaching women and controlling them, and be in quietness,' could that be justly construed as an interdiction of male preaching *for all time*, if once it were known that at that time special peril to men alone existed? Would not the use of such an expression as 'preachers of the Gospel' lead one to infer that when peace was restored these men would go back to the vocation named? So here; once knowing that special peril for women existed, the use of the expression '*women proclaiming godliness*' would merely indicate this as their normal occupation under normal conditions."

Moreover, Dr. Bushnell rightly observes, "the 'quietness' may be as much enjoined upon the one who is teaching as the one who is learning! It is not to be told abroad by either teacher or learner that the woman is *learning*. But yet the woman is to be allowed to learn. That was a step far in advance of the practice of the Jews."

Now follows one of the most glorious messages

from God to women to be found in the whole Bible but hidden from them, alas, for centuries, under mountains high of the misinterpretation of expositors. Let us dig out this "evangel," and see how it flashes with light from heaven.

The Apostle had just said, "*Let* a woman learn . . ." and then he goes on to give Timothy the reason why. His mind goes back to Eden, and he remembers how Eve through her innocence and immaturity had fallen a victim to the wiles of the devil and had become "thoroughly deceived" (lit. Greek), so he writes as follows—

Verses 13, 14 and 15: "*For Adam was first formed, then Eve; and Adam was not beguiled, but the woman being beguiled hath fallen into transgression: but she shall be saved through the childbearing, if they continue in faith and love and sanctification with sobriety.*" The word rendered "formed" here, points out Dr. Bushnell, is not the word used for "create." The Greek Lexicon says that its meaning is "to mould, form, shape." "The lesson Paul would draw from his reference to the beginning of the race is, that as Adam was first developed, and then Eve, in the natural world, so must it be in the social world." Adam "having been first formed, and hence being older than Eve, was not deceived." "Adam was not beguiled," said the Apostle. He sinned with his eyes open. But the woman was "*thoroughly* deceived." The one was a victim, the other a deliberate sinner.

Paul remembers the primeval promise that the woman's Seed should bruise the serpent's head. The victim of the serpent's wiles was dealt with in abounding grace and promised the honor of becoming the progenitor of a Saviour who would eventually destroy the serpent's power. She was saved *then*, through faith in a coming Saviour. How much more should she not be saved now, reasons the Apostle, when that Saviour had already come! And so he sets forth what may truly be described as the Magna Charta of womanhood. Yes, the woman in Eden was thoroughly deceived: but she shall be saved through the **childbearing** (of Jesus Christ) (cf. Gal. 4:4)! The childbearing—*the* great event of the world having its culmination at Calvary. The promise is clear. The woman "shall be saved" to the very full of all that the incarnation and death of the Son of God obtained for her. Woman is not for all time to remain under the shadow of Eve's "deception" any more than is the man to remain for all time under the shadow of Adam's willful sin. The woman *shall be saved"*; therefore, Timothy, *"let the woman learn. . ."* and learn of her re-demption from the Fall in the birth of the Saviour.

Ah, here we have the key to Satan's endeavor to fasten upon all women down the ages the results of his work in Eden. "The woman must not learn," said the Jews in Paul's time, and "the woman must not learn," said many of the theologians of the Christian Church, influenced by Judaism. "She was thoroughly deceived once," whispered the serpent, who, alas, has since extended his operations and thoroughly deceived the whole inhabited earth (Rev. 12:9). "See how the woman leads in all kinds of heretical movements today," cry some. "Is it not a proof that she is open to deception as much as she was in Eden?" Yes, it is undoubtedly true that on account of her greater spiritual capacity, the woman is more open to deception in the supernatural sphere just as men are more open to be thoroughly deceived in the intellectual realm. But is it not probable that women are being swept into the wiles of the devil today because the truths of God which they should have learned have been kept from them? Is it not because for centuries past they have not been given *the training in the Scriptures* which would have saved them and prepared them for the day of emancipation? Had the woman been encouraged to "learn" as the Apostle advised Timothy, might not her greater spiritual capacity have resulted in an accession of spiritual force to the church, which would have saved it from the deadly deception of the "Higher Criticism"?

Verse 15: "*But she shall be saved through the*

*childbearing, if they continue in faith and love
and sanctification with sobriety."*

The "if" here is important, for it gives the
conditions on the woman's part for the personal
realization of the promised salvation. The words
cover a wide scope in their meaning. "Faith"
in the Saviour, the "love" life of His indwelling,
the "sanctification" of spirit, soul and body, which
is the accompanying result of His salvation and,
in the practical life, the "self-restraint" (the
meaning of the Greek word translated "sobriety"), which is the outcome of recognizing that
the "body" is the temple of the Holy Ghost
(1 Cor. 19, 20).

Dr. Bushnell points out also that this "salvation" is not only spiritual but social. Paul implies,
she says, "that woman's social rescue began in
the birth of Jesus Christ," and "Christianity un-
hampered by the narrowness of man" purposed
to "raise woman until she stands on his level."
"She shall be saved through the childbearing
[of Jesus Christ]." This is the woman's evangel
and her message of hope to counter all the effects
of the Fall in Eden. Is it not strange that any
other meaning than their being the New Testament complement to the Gen. 3: 15 promise should
ever have been given to the words?[3] But woman's

---

3. We thankfully note that the R.V. gives Gal. 4:4 as the
marginal reference attached to these words.

emancipation day has come. Centuries of ignorance of the things of God have left their marks upon her; but women may "learn" at last, and men, too, will learn by the stern logic of experience that it has been a perilous policy for the Christian Church to have given a lower status to woman than that which was hers by right through the atoning work of the Son of God.

4

"Thou Art Turning . . . and . . ."

Now we must consider the most serious mistranslation in the English version of the Bible.
This mistranslation lies at the root of all the mis-
interpretations of the words of Paul in the New
Testament. Tears of blood would never avail to
wash away the tragic consequences to the womanhood of the world.

Dr. Bushnell's book devotes many pages to
the consideration of the subject, examining all
the Scriptures concerned and drawing upon the
facts of history. She shows the way in which in
the early centuries of the Christian era rabbinical
teaching gradually began to penetrate the Christian Church on this particular question until it
colored Christian theology the wide world over.

In these days of enlightenment and freedom
for women in general, we might see that we need

not trouble about the rendering of Gen. 3:16, except that we find a reference to it placed again and again in the margins of the New Testament, showing that the fundamental mistranslation in Genesis perpetually colored the minds of translators in interpreting the language of St. Paul. For instance, we find in one version of the New Testament a note in the margin of 1 Cor. 11:3, saying, "*cf. Gen. 3:16. The woman's veil, or head covering, is a symbol of this subordination*"; again in 1 Cor. 14:34, a marginal reference says, "*cf. Gen. 3:16*"; and yet again in 1 Tim. 2:11, to the word "subjection" is placed the reference "*cf. Gen 3:16.*" All showing that Gen. 3:16 is supposed to interpret the words of Paul in these particular passages in the New Testament.

It is necessary, therefore, to turn to this passage and show how seriously this verse has been mistranslated, so that its sinister influence upon the interpretation of the language of Paul may be destroyed.

The Revised Version gives the verse in Gen. 3:16 as follows:

> Unto the woman he said, I will greatly multiply thy sorrow and thy conception; in sorrow thou shalt bring forth children; and thy desire shall be to thy husband, and he shall rule over thee.

We cannot attempt to give but a fraction of

the light thrown by Dr. Bushnell on the whole passage in the original Hebrew. She lays firm foundations for her statements by first giving explanations and examples of the form of the Hebrew characters, so that all students of her lessons might understand what is generally known only by Hebrew scholars. She explains the minute care taken by the Jews in transcribing their scriptures, so that the "original text has been preserved in MSS. with scarcely an important change." She knows the difference between "lawful" and "unlawful" textual criticism, the one being a lawful examination of the work of transcribers and translators and the latter a manipulation of the text itself; she carefully distinguishes between the original text of the Bible as "inspired, infallible and inviolable," and *translations* of the Bible as necessarily open to question where they do not accurately give the sense of the original.[1]

All this is important for proving the statements upon which such vital issues depend; for it will be seen, as we go further, how different is the meaning of Gen. 3:16 from that which has been given to it by commentators for centuries of the Christian era.

---

1. Conybeare and Howson's "Epistles of St. Paul"—the classic upon the subject—with their valuable footnotes, illustrates the way in which the English text can be legitimately examined by the Bible student.

The greatest and most grievous mistranslation in the verse is the word translated in the R.V. "desire," for in its correct rendering the whole meaning of the passage is changed.

The word in Hebrew, says Dr. Bushnell, is used only three times in the Old Testament—in Gen. 3:16, 4:7, and Song of Solomon 7:10. "The original word is *teshuqa*, and as it only occurs three times in the Hebrew Bible, its sense must be fixed, (1) by studying its relation to other words in the sentences where it occurs, (2) by studying its derivation and structure, (3) by studying the way it is rendered in the ancient versions of Scripture."

Dr. Bushnell shows the use of the word in the following simple way:

> Gen. 3:16, "and-to-Adam." Eve's *"teshuqa."*
> Gen. 4:7, "and-to-Cain." Abel's *"teshuqa."*
> S. S. 7:10, "and-to-the-church." *Christ's "teshuqa."*

What is said (typically) of Christ must have the same meaning in Abel or Eve! But what do the ancient versions say? How do they translate *"teshuqa"*? We find that every version up to one hundred years after Christ, e.g., the Septuagint Greek, the Syriac Peshito, the Samaritan and Old Latin, all render the word as "turning." God said that Eve was "turning" to Adam; that Abel was "turning" to Cain, and (Song of Solomon 10) that Christ is "turning" toward His Bride, the church.

The meanings are obviously the same.

But this is not all of the amazing truth. The Hebrew word which has been rendered "conception" in this verse in English is not the one usually used for that word[2] in the Hebrew language, for it is *two letters short*. One scholar says "it is an abnormal formation, which occurs nowhere else in the Old Testament." And a very high lexical authority calls it a "contraction or erroneous." So in translating the very words of God—upon which the lives of millions of the human race depended— some translators have added two missing letters to a word which they describe as a "contraction" instead of translating it *exactly as it was written*, when it would give the meaning of "sighing."

That this is correct is proved by the fact that the Septuagint Greek version, which is the first and oldest translation of the Hebrew Bible, renders the word *"sighing"* as it is in the original. The word "sorrow," too, in the same sentence as well as in the following one, is the one used of Adam in the next verse, and so it can have no special and peculiar application to Eve as a woman.

And yet here is another revelation of far-reaching import in this extraordinarily misinter-

---

2. The word occurs in Ruth 4:13, Hosea 9:11, and nowhere else, and is correctly translated in these passages.—*Dr. Bushnell*

preted text. The words *shall be* in the last section of the verse are in italics in the A.V. and therefore admittedly not in the original Hebrew. Eve's "turning" to Adam was not the result of a "shall" —preordained of God. Nor was its result the outcome of a "shall." "And he *will* rule over thee," said the Omniscient Jehovah as He foresaw what the consequences would be.

If no "shall" rule is to be found in the Hebrew original, and "all the ancient versions testify that the verb is a simple future," therefore no "*rule*" was preordained by God. The words contained "a warning and a prophecy," writes Dr. Bushnell, "of what has been abundantly fulfilled, . . . especially in heathen lands." Dr. Bushnell says, too, "If it be contended that the context proves . . . an imperative, then the previous sentences must be imperative": "*Must* the serpent bruise the heel of the woman's Seed, whether he will or no! *Must* man rule woman whether he will or no?"

Now with these facts in mind, let us read Gen. 3:16 as Dr. Bushnell renders it:

> Unto the woman he said, A snare hath increased thy sorrow and thy sighing; in sorrow shalt thou bring forth children; thou art turning to thy husband, and he will rule over thee.

We don't have space for giving Dr. Bushnell's reasons for using the expression "a snare"; but it takes us back to verse 15 which contains the

Evangel Promise to the woman, that through her should come a Seed who would finally crush the serpent who had caused her fall. The primary point which we need to grasp is the fact that the text as it stands in the original Hebrew does not contain a "law" of preordained subordination of woman, such as is suggested by its use in New Testament margins; and, incidentally, it is thereby proved that words "as saith the law" used in 1 Cor. 14:34 do not refer to Gen. 3:16. "Rule" there would be, the Lord himself said, but not a "rule" ordained by Him to be perpetuated as a "commandment of the Lord" in the Christian Church in the time to come.

The most heart-stirring point of all in Dr. Bushnell's exegesis of the whole passage is the way it is made clear that Eve went forth from Eden not "cursed" but a forgiven and restored believer, "elevated in her own person" to the "honourable position of an enemy of Satan," and constituted "the progenitor of the coming destroyer of Satan and his power."

The reason for this is to be found in Eve's answer to Jehovah when she was asked what she had done, for her reply really involved a "choice" and an exposure of the character of Satan when she said that he had "beguiled her." By doing this, she "created an enmity between herself and him," which God confirmed in His words to Satan,

"I will put enmity between thee and the woman."
Dr. Monroe Gibson says, "There is, properly
speaking, no present tense in Hebrew—only the
past and future. . . . So here, it is not only 'I will
put enmity;' but 'I am putting, and will put' enmity between thee and the woman. The work is
begun . . . She is the first type and representa-
tive of all the separated ones who constitute the
church of God." In brief, writes Dr. Bushnell,
God said in effect, "She has chosen to make the
breach; I will widen it."

This is a justifiable conclusion if we think of
all that must have passed through the mind of
Eve when she heard the voice of God in the Garden. She realized that the serpent had deceived
her and when asked, said so, without shrinking
from the certain result of arousing his enmity
against her. She chose to speak the truth, and
thereby began that enmity, which Jehovah confirmed as a special prerogative for herself and
her (spiritual) Seed after her. This fixed enmity
of the serpent accounted largely "for a whole
train of evils, prophesied" in verse 16, concerning
her after-path in life, for, Dr. Bushnell points
out, "*God nowhere says that Eve's sorrowful and
oppressed part is 'because' she had done anything*," and as the words of the Lord to Eve, in
verse 16, so closely follow upon those spoken to
the serpent in verse 15, "we have sufficient reason

for concluding that all '*this*' might result" through the enmity of Satan.

But what ground is there for saying that Eve became a "believer," the first believer on Jesus Christ restored to fellowship with the God she had disobeyed?

The clue is hidden in the original Hebrew of Gen. 4:1. Eve gives evidence that she believed in God's promise of a coming Victor over Satan when on the birth of her firstborn she exclaims, "I have gotten a man—*even the Coming One.*" Canon Payne Smith says about this exclamation of Eve, "Jehovah means literally 'He will come,' that is, 'The Coming One.' The name is really man's answer to and acceptance of the promise made in Gen. 3:15; and why should not Eve, *to whom the promise was given, be the first to profess faith in it?* . . . For her faith's sake, the spirit of prophecy rested upon her, and she gave Him on whom her hopes were fixed the title which was to grow and swell onward till all inspired truth gathered round it . . ."—the name Jehovah, which is the New Testament name "Lord."

That Eve believed God and His promise of a Saviour, and that it was "counted to her for righteousness" as much as to Abraham in later years, is to be seen also in the name which Adam gave her after their interview with God (cf. Gen. 3:20), and just before Jehovah himself clothed

them with the skins of animals slain, preparatory
to their leaving the Garden.

Let us turn again to the story. The verdict
on Adam concluded with the words "dust thou
art, and unto dust shalt thou return" (Gen. 3:19),
which was a verdict of *death*. But at once we
read, "And the man called his wife's name 'Eve'
[that is, *living*, or *life*, R.V.m.], because she
was the mother of all living." That is, writes
Dr. Bushnell, "marking the contrast between himself and Eve, Adam called his wife 'Eve'—'living'—*spiritually* living," and all believers are the
"seed of the woman" in Christ—not merely "mankind." Delitzsch remarks about these words of
Adam, "The promise purports truly a 'seed of
the woman.' In the very face . . . of the death with
which he is threatened, the wife is for Adam the
security for both . . ." On the point as to all *believers* being the "seed of the woman," Dr. Monroe Gibson asks, "Who are her seed?" and re-
plies, "In a certain sense, of course, all mankind
are 'seed of the woman,' but suppose you include
all mankind, where do the seed of the serpent
come in? [with whom her seed are at enmity].
Is it not quite obvious that the 'seed of the woman'
cannot mean all mankind but simply those . . .
who are found . . . on the side of God and righteousness? Those who are of an opposite spirit

are the seed of the serpent, the 'children of the devil.' "

But what about the prevalent idea that Eve was cursed and punished for her fall into the snare set forth for her? (1 Tim. 2:14). In the Scripture itself there is no curse mentioned as passed either upon Adam or Eve, but only upon the serpent and the ground; nor "does God lay any charge of express disobedience at the door of Eve." Dr. Bushnell exhaustively treats in several lessons the historical causes for the false doctrine of "the curse on Eve," clearly showing that it has penetrated into Christian theology from the Babylonian Talmud which appeared in 800 A.D.[3] in which is recorded the fable of "Ten curses against Eve," most of these being unfit for quotation. The earliest source was a pagan Greek myth which is recorded about 800 B.C. This came into Jewish teaching at a time called in Jewish history the "days of mingling"—the period of four hundred years between the close of the Old Testament and the opening of the New Testament—when the Jews tried to reconcile Jewish customs and the teachings of the Old Testament with Greek paganism.

---

3. Dr. Bushnell says she gives this date on the authority of Prof. Margoliouth of Oxford. It has often been fixed as early as 300 A.D.

72

As we ponder over the painful story we do
not wonder that Dr. Bushnell says, "The teaching
that God punishes Christian women for the sin
of Eve, is a wicked and cruel superstition, and
unworthy the intelligence of Christians," and, in
addition to this, it has laid "a blighting hand upon
woman's self-respect, self-confidence and spiritual activity, from which causes the entire church
of Jesus Christ suffers moral and spiritual loss."

This brings us to the question as to how the
mistranslation of Gen. 3:16 has crept into our English versions of the Scriptures if the Hebrew word
teshuqa was always translated "turning" in all
versions of the Old Testament up to at least 200
years after Christ.⁴ Dr. Bushnell has devoted two
lessons, together with a valuable chart, to making
clear these vital facts, but we cannot attempt,
even to summarize, the evidences she has collect-
ed with such painstaking research. The chart
shows all the versions of the Scriptures with the
dates when they were made and their various
translations of the word *teshuqa*, right through
the centuries down to the present time. The Latin

<hr />

4. Dr. Bushnell adds a note pointing out that the Church
Fathers seem to be ignorant of any other sense but "turning"
for the word *teshuqa*, e.g., Clement of Rome, Irenaeus, Tertullian, Origen, Epiphanius, Jerome, Ambrose, Augustine,
Theodoret, all employ "turning" in one, two, or all three passages.

Vulgate, a version made under rabbinical influence in 282 A.D., rendered the word as "power"
instead of "turning." And from it, and *not direct
from the original Hebrew, the first English version* by Wycliffe, published in 1380, was made.
Then after Wycliffe's version and before any other
English Bible appeared an Italian monk named
Pagnino (or Pagnimus, *Latin*) translated the Hebrew Bible into Latin in 1528, and he was the
first who translated *teshuqa* into the misleading
and unjustifiable rendering which strangely has
colored all the English versions to the present
time (with the exception of Wycliffe's Bible, already mentioned, and the Douay Bible, both of
which were made direct from the Latin Vulgate
of 282 A.D.). It was seven years after Pagnino's
version was published at Lyons that Coverdale's
English Bible appeared, and Tyndale's Bible in
the time between—both of which were published
on the Continent, this probably accounting, says
Dr. Bushnell, for their being influenced by Pagnino. At any rate, she says, *"from the time Pagnino's version appeared, every English version*
(except the two Vulgate referred to) *has followed
Pagnino's rendering"* of Gen. 3:16 up to the present day.

This is enough to show the necessity for a different translation and interpretation of Gen. 3:16,
although, observes Dr. Bushnell, the need "will

scarcely be realised by those familiar with the usual teachings in our Bible Commentaries, which defy principles of morality and justice," as well as "outrage the sense of the original words, as proved by the ancient versions."

5

Some Misunderstood Words

Now let us return to the New Testament and briefly examine some of the words used by the Apostle Paul to which we find attached in the margin a reference to Gen. 3:16, notwithstanding that *Paul's language applied only to women who were Christians*, in the New Testament sense of being a Christian, i.e., born of the Spirit and partakers of the divine nature, or "a new creation in Christ Jesus"—members of the Body of Christ, drawn out of all classes, from every tongue and tribe and nation.

Subjection

First let us take the word "subjection" in 1 Cor. 14:34, which verse, we have already seen, contains a quotation of the words of the Judaizers

76

at Corinth. There was one sentence in their language which contained the truth, for they probably had heard Paul speak again and again of the duty of Christian subjection. But used by the Judaizers it was "truth" strained to suit their own purposes, for believing as they did in the Oral Law and imbued with its teaching about the subordination of woman, we may judge that they did not mean what Paul meant when they made use of the word "subjection." *They* meant subordination, but Paul meant something quite different. An examination of the word in the original throws some light on this. Dr. Bushnell points out that "the verb 'to be in subjection' is from *hupo*, meaning 'next after,' or 'under'; and *tasso*—'arrange,' meaning 'to arrange after,' or 'arrange under,' as soldiers are arranged, file after file, or under a captain."

The way in which the Apostle Paul used the word may be seen by consideration of all its connections in his epistles and the various kinds of persons to whom he applied it. "The noun 'subjection,'" says Dr. Bushnell, "is not found in the Greek language outside of the New Testament." Therefore it is reasonable *"to infer that it was coined to describe a relation peculiar to believers."* It is also noteworthy that the A.V. often translates the Greek word in question as "obey" and "submit," but the R.V. carefully renders it as "subjection," and "be in subjection," wherever it occurs, thus "distinguishing them in their sense from obedience." (Compare the A.V. and R.V. in 1 Cor. 14:34 and Titus 2:5.)

The true sense of the word, says Dr. Bushnell, describes "the Christian grace of yielding one's preferences to another where no principle is involved, rather than asserting one's rights. Schleusner's Greek-Latin Lexicon to the Septuagint says that this verb does not always 'convey the thought of servile subjection.' Jesus, as a boy, was 'subject' to His parents, yet we know that He did not even consult them when about His Father's business." The use of the word in other connections in the New Testament shows that this meaning of subjection is correct and that Gen. 3:16, with its supposed "law" of "subordination" to "rule," is not a true interpretation of its purport *when applied only to women..*

Let us look at a few of the other instances where the word is used. In Eph. 5:21, R.V., we read *"subjecting yourselves one to another* in the fear of Christ." Here we have an admonition written to all Christians irrespective of sex. Again in 1 Pet. 5:5, A.V., *"all of you be subject* one to another . . ."; and in 1 Cor. 16:16 the Apostle urges the Roman Christians to be in "subjection" unto everyone that "helpeth in the work" (some of these being women as shown by Rom. 16:3

and 12). In Eph. 5:22, R.V., the words "be in subjection" are in italics, showing that they are not in the original, yet in the R.V. margin to these very words we find the reference "see Gen. 3:16." Omitting the italics the sentence would read, "Wives, unto your husbands, as unto the Lord," obviously taking its sense from the previous verse inculcating the "subjection" of believers one to another, the "subjection" being in "wives" the very same kind of grace to be manifested in all.

In Col. 3:18 and Titus 2:5 we have again "subjection" enjoined upon wives, as is "fitting in the Lord"—in each case the Greek word being the same as rendered "subjection one to another." Again this shows that the meaning of New Testament "subjection" is not the "rule" of Gen. 3:16, which Eve fell under because of her own turning to Adam and not by the preordination of God. This rule therefore does not originate from the Holy Ghost as a manifestation of the Spirit of Christ and may be incidentally evidenced by the fact that "to the extent that grace works in the heart of the husband, he loses his . . . desire to 'rule' his wife"—and, *vice versa*, any "rule" of the husband by the wife is an anomaly never suggested in the Scriptures! "Subjection" one to another is therefore a grace of the Spirit and a manifestation of the law of courtesy which should be seen as operative between sons and daughters of the Lord Almighty, who always say the one to the other, "You first—I gladly go 'next after.' "

Obedience

It is important to distinguish between the use of the words "subjection" and "obedience." They are different in the Greek, and the R.V. has therefore changed the words of the A.V. "obey" and "submit" into "subjection" wherever the Greek word for the latter is used in the original. It is striking that the word "obey" is used only in relation to servants and always for children but invariably the word "subjection" for wives; with one exception, 1 Pet. 3:6, where the Apostle Peter points women to the example of Sarah, who "obeyed Abraham, calling him Lord" or "Sir." On the other hand, in Gen. 21:12, God bade Abraham "obey" Sarah's voice when she said what was right, showing that the "relation of obedience and respect" was mutual and reciprocal a n d based only upon the question of "right" and not of sex.

This distinction, brought out so clearly by the R.V., between "subjection" and "obedience,"[1] is very important, and the fact that the former word

---

1. This also throws light on Rom. 13:1, as not in contradiction to Acts 5:29, i.e., "subjection"—a conciliatory spirit, does not imply "obedience" to anything contrary to the known will of God.

has never been interpreted as meaning or including obedience, when it is used in the relation of man to man, is sufficient to free its use from the idea of servility or subordination. The New Testament meaning of "yielding preferences" one to the other in conciliation and loving self-sacrifice, every Christian, man and woman, will admit is a necessity for order and arrangement in the affairs of life, as well as being an expression of Christian character, which is well-pleasing to God.

Headship

Again we find the marginal reference Gen. 3:16 attached to the words in 1 Cor. 11:3, "the head of the woman is the man." But we must not forget that "at Corinth the church used the Septuagint Greek version, and would read Gen. 3:16 as 'Thou art *turning* to thy husband, and he 'will' rule over thee.'" So it would not convey to the Christians at Corinth what it does in our day. "Now had we always read Gen. 3:16," writes Dr. Bushnell, "'he *will* rule over thee' instead of 'he *shall* rule over thee' and known that the verb is a simple future (as all ancient versions testify), ignorant, careless, or dishonest interpreters centuries ago would not have thought to show that this rule was God-ordained. . . . We question, then, the correctness of placing Gen. 3:16 against the words 'of a wife the husband is the head,' as interpreting it to mean, 'of the wife the husband is the *ruler.*'"

But what is the New Testament meaning of the "headship" of the husband? (*Not, let us notice, of "man" over "woman"* in general, as the use of the word *aner* (husband) in 1 Cor. 11:3-14, makes clear.) Dr. Bushnell devotes an entire lesson to showing the use of the word "head" in the Old Testament, but we can look only briefly at her clear explanation of the word in the New Testament as interpreted for the Christian— and *only the Christian*—by the analogy of Christ as the Head of the Church. She asks in what sense Christ is described as "head" to His Church. Then he points out that Col. 2:19 describes it most fully. He is "the head, from which all the body by joints and bands having nourishment ministered, and knit together, increaseth with the increase of God." Neither here nor in Eph. 4:15 is Christ's government referred to but His headship as the support, nourishment and builder of the Body. In Eph. 1:22, His headship as a "rule" is clear, but this is over principalities and powers (see Eph. 1:21, 22), which are placed under His feet. But we are never told that this is the place for His Church! God gave Him to be "head over all things to the church which is his body, the fulness of him that filleth all in all." The place of the Church is then shown as "raised up with him," and made to "sit with him," to *share in his rule* over the "all things" placed under His feet (Eph. 2:6).

It was true in those days, says Dr. Bushnell, that the husband was ahead of his wife, but this made it all the more obligatory upon him that he should also be a "head" after the pattern of Christ, to support and lift up his wife to his own level. The words of Eph. 5:33 concerning this obligation are very beautiful in the original. They read, "Let every one of you in particular, so love his wife even as himself, *in order that* [expressed in Greek by a single Greek word denoting design] the wife may *reverence* [or revere] her husband." This is the key to "headship." The true "headship" is won by self-sacrificing love, even as Christ won His Church—not by rule and domination but by laying down His life for her. Reverence is gained by love; it can never be demanded as a right, nor created in the one who is to give it in any other way than by being "ahead" in manifesting the character of Christ. Therefore in the Church of Christ "even as Christ" (Eph. 5:23) is the meaning of the headship described by the Apostle Paul—a headship which most truly shows forth the divine pattern of Christ and His Church.

Diakonos

There are also some other misunderstood

words in the New Testament in connection with
the work and status of Christian women in the
early church, showing that in translating other
parts of scripture bearing upon the subject, the
minds of the translators have always been colored
by Gen. 3:16 and the supposed teaching of Paul
in the three obscure passages on the position of
women to which we have referred. Dr. Bushnell
points out an instance of this bias of mind: the
rendering into English of the Greek word *diakonos*
whenever it occurs in connection with women's
ministry. The word occurs, she says, thirty times
in the New Testament and is almost always rendered "minister." It is translated seven times
as "servant," three times as "deacon," and
twenty times as "minister."[2] It may, or certainly
does, refer to an ecclesiastical office, as in Phil.
1:1, and 1 Tim. 3:8, 12, where it is rendered
"deacon." But in Rom. 16:1 where Paul says,
"I commend unto you Phoebe, our sister, who
is *diakonos* of the church which is at Cenchrea,"
the translators render it as "servant" (A.V.), the
R.V. margin giving it as "deaconess."

Bishop Lightfoot, speaking of the translation
of *diakonos* as "servant," gives strong reasons
for believing that 1 Tim. 3:11 refers to women
deacons and says, "If the testimony borne in these

---

2. Rom. 15:8; 1 Cor. 3:5; 2 Cor. 3:6, 6:4, 11:23; Eph. 3:7,
6:21; Col. 1:7, 23, 25, 4:7; 1 Thess. 3:2; 1 Tim. 4:6.

two passages to a ministry of women in Apostolic times, had not thus been blotted out of our English Bibles, . . . our English Church would not have been maimed of one of her hands." As to the R.V. margin rendering the word as "deaconess," Bishop Ellicott says that this is open to the objection that "it introduces into the New Testament the technical name *diakonissa*, which is of later origin"; *it is not the word which Paul himself used.* So the fact remains that the Apostle described Phoebe as a *"deacon,"* not a "deaconess" —a "minister" of the church, using the very same word as in 1 Tim. 3:8, 12—this fact going a long way, observes Dr. Bushnell, "toward proving that when he gave directions as to ordaining 'deacons' he made no distinction as to sex in his own mind."

6

Some Glimpses into History

We have space in our concluding chapters only briefly to say that one primary fact emerges from all the light upon Gen. 3:16 and the information brought together by Dr. Bushnell in her textbook. And that is that in the early period of the human race and less and less down to the time between the Old Testament and the New Testament story —a period of 400 years, called in Jewish history the "days of mingling"—woman had a very different status from that which she is seen to occupy among the Jews in the days of Paul and a different position also from that which she held in the Christian Church after the early centuries of the Christian era.

All the facts of history referred to by Dr. Bushnell on this point will be a revelation to those who know nothing about them. Professor Flinders

Petrie says that women were heads of their
tribes in Abraham's day, for Sarah's name was
changed to the "well understood title of a female
prince" (Gen. 17:15, 16), or "chieftainess." He
writes, "Sar" is "the regular old term for a chief,
still kept up in the East, [and Sarah's] position
. . . was not by any means that of secluded de-
pendence, but rather that of an independent head,
or tribal mother." In those days there were
matriarchs [1] as well as patriarchs, and kinship
was reckoned through the women and not the
men. Professor Sayce writes that Sumeria, Ak
Kadia, Babylonia, Arabia, Phoenicia and Egypt
were all ancient civilizations "characterized by
features of the matriarchy," and Prof. Ramsay
says "the best authenticated cases of 'Mutter-
rect' [2] belong to Asia Minor." Also in Genesis 36
we discover that some of the "dukes of Edom"
were women, and we have an interesting sidelight
in the meaning of the name of Dinah as "the
female judge."

It is now conceded also by Bible scholars,
writes Dr. Bushnell, that women had their place
in the Tabernacle services either as Priestess or
Levite, as "proved by the technical term used
in Ex. 38:8 and 1 Sam. 2:22." But the reluctance

---

1. I.e., Matriarchism, rule by women.

2. Mother rule.

of Jewish translators to translate the original faithfully when it ran across their prejudices connected with the position of women is to be found even in the Septuagint Greek version, for the translators, who were Jews, rendered the Hebrew word as "fasting women" in Ex. 38:8 and omitted the entire phrase containing the words in 1 Sam. 2:22. Prof. Margoliouth, of Oxford, comments on this: "It is evident that by the time when the Septuagint translation was made, the idea of women ministering at the door of the Tabernacle had become so odious *that it was wilfully mistranslated.*"

The early dignity of woman is therefore unmistakably to be traced in the Old Testament Scriptures; and Kalisch, the Bible expositor, allows that they were in those days admitted to the highest office of teaching, that of prophets —Miriam, Deborah, and Huldah.[3] He comments on the seemingly narrower sphere allotted to women under the Gospel. But the light we have now gained does not indicate that a narrower sphere was allotted to women in the Christian dispensation. If there are no Deborahs referred to in the

3. Read the account of Miriam (Ex. 15:20); of Deborah (Judg. chap. 4 and 5); of Huldah (2 Kings 22); the references to women who "prophesy out of their own heart" (Ezek. 3:17), implying the existence of many women prophets who were not false.—Dr. Bushnell

New Testament, or Huldahs as "judges," is it not because God adapts His messengers to the age or dispensation in which they live? There was no Moses going up the fiery mount in apostolic days, but there was a Paul who was equally a revelator of God's will to his age as Moses was in his. The Judaizers described Paul's "bodily presence" as "weak, and his speech contemptible," and to people of his day and generation he probably appeared far below Moses in his service, but afterwards he is seen to have been to the Christian Church what Moses was to the people of God in the wilderness.

Even so it can be with the Deborahs and Huldahs of the Apostolic Age and in every age. There are traces in history of women's ministry in apostolic days as well as those recorded in the Scriptures, although on account of the teaching of the Jews and the deadening influences of the Oral Law upon them, women were far behind the men in education. But we cannot forget that this would not prevent the Holy Spirit *teaching them the deep things of God*, which the "natural man," however highly educated, could not know.

We have as examples some notable women referred to in the letters of Paul, which show that they did teach when the Spirit of God made them capable of doing so. Phoebe we have already mentioned, but there is more to say about her.

Conybeare and Howson, in their *Life of St. Paul,*
call attention to the use in Paul's recommenda-
tion of her of two words associated together
in technical legal matters, which indicate that
she was abroad on some important business
with the Courts—possibly in behalf of the church.
"What Paul says of Phoebe," writes Dr. Bushnell, "as a *prostatis* (translated 'succourer,'
literally meaning 'one standing before'), proves
that she was of no inferior order in the church."
The word means in Greek a champion, leader,
chief, protector, patron! It is the "noun form
corresponding to the verb translated 'rule' in
1 Tim. 3:4, 5, 12 and 5:17. But it could not be
translated as if Paul said 'she hath been a "ruler"
of many, and of myself also!' The fact is," Dr.
Bushnell says, "that the passages in Timothy
referred to do not speak of 'rule.'" In Titus 3:8,
14, the word is translated "maintain," and
*Phoebe held the same relation to the Church at
Cenchrea* that Paul says, "church officials"
should hold to their own children and household
—take good care of them! Theodoret says, writes
Mrs. Booth, "The fame of Phoebe was spoken
of throughout the world. She was known not only
to the Greeks and Romans, but also to the Bar-
barians," which "implies that she had travelled
much, and propagated the Gospel in foreign coun-
tries."

We have also referred elsewhere to Priscilla, and there is more to say about her and her work in the early church. The first reference to Priscilla is to be found in Acts 18:2, where we read of Paul's arrival at Corinth. He there met Aquila and his wife Priscilla, "lately come from Italy," and took up his abode with them. After eighteen months in Corinth, Paul and Priscilla and Aquila removed to Ephesus. Here came, later on, Apollos, a "learned man," "mighty in the Scriptures," but spiritually "knowing only the baptism of John." And "when Priscilla and Aquila heard him, they took him unto them, and expounded unto him the way of God more carefully." Here we find Priscilla as a "teacher." She was one who evidently had been taught of God so deeply that she could spiritually instruct a man "mighty in the Scriptures," and this was not a small thing when said about a Jew. "There are certain indications," says Dean Alford, "that [Aquila] was rather the ready and zealous patron than the teacher; and this latter work, or a great share of it, seems to have belonged to his wife Priscilla." Another expositor says that "she must have been associated with, and more distinguished than, her husband. . . . One is allowed to infer . . . that she was the chief instructor, otherwise she would scarcely have been mentioned." In Rom. 16:3, Paul calls her and Aquila his "fellow-labourers."

"This expression," writes Dr. Bushnell, "not so very frequently employed by Paul, means much. By its use Priscilla and Aquila are legitimatized official Evangelists and Teachers." It is noteworthy also that after the first instance in Acts 18:1, Priscilla is always mentioned first (Acts 18:18, 26, R.V.; Rom. 16:3; 2 Tim. 4:19) with the single exception of 1 Cor. 16:19. It is therefore a historical fact that Priscilla is associated in the period of her greatest activity with the Apostle at the very time that he is represented by expositors as relegating women to silence.

Then we are told in Acts 2:9 that "Phillip, the evangelist, had four daughters, virgins, which did prophesy." The ancient church historian Eusebius says that these godly women fulfilled the work of evangelists, "to preach Christ to those who had never yet heard the word of the faith, and to deliver to them the record of the Holy Gospels." He also refers to Potomania Ammias, a prophetess in Philadelphia, and others "who were equally distinguished for their love and zeal in the cause of Christ."

There is also a reference to women "apostles" in Rom. 16:7; Paul writes, "Salute Andronicus and Junia, my kinsmen, and my fellow-prisoners, who are of note among the apostles." Chrysostom and Theophylact, both Greeks, "say Junia was a woman; 'kinsmen' should therefore have been

rendered 'kinsfolk,' " writes Mrs. Booth. She
also says, "Justin Martyr, who lived until about
A.D. 150, says, in his dialogue with Trypho the
Jew, that 'both men and women were seen among
them who had the extraordinary gifts of the Spirit
of God, according as the prophet Joel had fore-
told." And Dodwell, in his Dissertions of Irenaeus,
says that "the gift of the spirit of prophecy was
given to others besides the Apostles: and that
not only in the first and second, but in the third
century—even to the time of Constantine—men
had these gifts; yea, and *women* too."

"Women's only century in the Christian
Church," observes Dr. Bushnell, "was during
Apostolic days, and a little while thereafter,"
although there are records that there were wom-
en teachers and preachers during the first four
centuries. In an article in the *Indian Standard*
(the organ of the Presbyterian Church in India),
a writer on "Women Preachers" gives the following instances of their work in the early centuries
of Christianity:

(1) "Tertullian, one of the earliest of the Latin
fathers, notes that women appear in every early
reference to ecclesiastical orders. Four titles,"
he writes, "are applied to the women clergy, all
of which occur in the New Testament, 'Widow,'
'Deaconess,' 'Presbyter,' 'Virgin.' The two former," he adds, "are Apostolic orders.

(2) "Marcella preached Christianity publicly in Rome, and Jerome (born about 340 A.D., and the translator of the Latin Vulgate Bible), writes of her: 'all that I learn with great study . . . the blessed Marcella learnt also but with great facility.' He also celebrates her immense influence for good in Rome.

(3) "In the Catacombs are found representations of women clergy, and they are shown presiding at the Lord's Supper. . . .

(4) "Mabillon, a French writer on ecclesiastical biography and antiquities, records that the evangelisation of Europe was due in great part to the Nuns of St. Benedict, many of whom publicly preached the Gospel.

(5) "Among the Montanists,[4] who were the evangelicals of the third century, Priscilla and Maximilla, ladies of rank, served as evangelists over a wide extent of country. Women were elected by the Montanists as Deacons, Pastors, President-Presbyters or Bishops. Opinions vary as to when the recognized order of women clergy died out. All agree that it lingered longer in the East

---

4. The Montanists took their name from Montanus, who claimed to be a divinely commissioned prophet and the bearer of a fresh influx of the Spirit. Some say that he "called himself the Paraclete." Tertullian joined the Montanists, who were loyal to the fundamental truths of the Gospel. They proclaimed the imminent return of Christ and demanded the radical reform of the church.

than in the West. . . ." "It seems," says the writer, "as if the decay of women's ministry took place with the decay of Christianity, the rise of the Roman Apostasy, and the proud pretensions of an exclusive priesthood."

But Dr. Bushnell's book throws much light upon this very question—a light that is important at the present time because it shows that it was *only when the teachings of the Jewish Rabbis began to influence the translations of the Scriptures* that the status of Christian women in the church was changed. This means that the "Judaism" which Paul the Apostle so successfully combated in its efforts to fasten circumcision upon the Christians of his time did eventually succeed in robbing the church of the active ministry of women.

In this light a comparison of the dates of the various translations made during the Christian era is very significant. Dean Stanley says that the Septuagint Greek was "the Bible of the Evangelists, and the Apostles of the first century, and of the Christian church for the first age of its existence, and was the text sanctioned probably by our Lord Himself."

Then in the second century, points out Dr. Bushnell, three Greek versions of the Hebrew Scriptures were made by the Jews and Judaizers *"with the express object of emphasizing the teaching of the Jews where they differed from Christianity.*" Following these, in the year 382, appeared the Latin Vulgate, translated by Jerome, who went to Palestine and studied Hebrew under the Jewish Rabbis, imbibing naturally the rabbinical viewpoint of the original Scriptures. Then came in the fourth century the tremendous change in the status of the "church" itself, when Constantine the Great took it under his protection. From this time on we have the gradual rise of an exclusive priesthood and an ecclesiastical system which has led men further and further away from the simplicity of the early days of Christianity.

7

Conclusion

It only remains now in conclusion to summarize the purpose of the issue of this edition in addition to what has been said in the introduction.

First and foremost, our purpose in cooperating with Dr. Bushnell in making known to Christian women the truths which God has enabled her to gain for His redeemed church is that we see it is impossible for the invisible church, consisting of the living members of Christ, to reach "full stature" in preparation for the Lord's return unless each member of the "Body," set in its place by God, fulfills its office. For how can the Body reach full growth, and "make increase with the increase of God," if some of its members are quenching the Spirit or retarding their own growing up into Christ by breaking the laws of the Spirit in His leading them on into maturity?

It has been said that this question of the status of Christian women and their right to speak or pray in the assembly of saints most vitally concerns the Body of Christ; and this is so, for if a member of the Body, in which Paul says there cannot be "male or female," fails to carry out the will of the "Head," *it checks the life of the entire Body and the manifestation of the Spirit through all its members.*

It is important for the understanding of this to distinguish (1) the "church" as an organization (in various sections) of professing Christians and (2) the "church" as an organism forming the mystical Body of Christ. In the first are rules and laws made by men who have a right to say who shall and who shall not occupy certain places and do certain work in its services; and Christian principle demands that no woman, or man for that matter, should act contrary to these rules. In the second—the "church" as an organism, formed of living members of Christ—are the "laws of the Spirit," which govern members of the Body according to the will of the Head; and each member must be free to obey the Spirit if the Body of Christ is to increase with the increase of God.

In Paul's description of the assembly in 1 Cor. 14, the principles of action for the members of the Body—the "church" as an organism—are

easily to be seen in their external manifestation
as they worked out in the early church—and as
they would work out today if the Spirit of God
had right of way in the gatherings of God's people.

It is this difference between the professing
church of the present time and the mystical
"church" [Body] of Christ which Christian women
need to understand in their service for Christ
when, under the guidance of the Holy Spirit, they
are called to "proclaim godliness." *Where* and
when they are to speak, the Spirit of God must
show them. But *they should clearly define on what
footing they stand as they speak.* If they are to
have working with them the Holy Spirit, do they
speak as women or from their *spiritual* position
as members of the Body of Christ, "new crea-
tions" in Him?

This point is so vital for the obtaining of the
co-working of the Holy Spirit in service that we
must endeavor to make it clear. Let us turn for
illustration to Eph. 2:11-19, where Paul speaks of
the cause of the enmity between Jew and Gentile
as "the laws of commandments contained in ordinances." This enmity, the Apostle says, was slain
through the cross so that "He might create in himself of the twain one new man"—the Body of
Christ of which He is the Head. On the Cross,
where the old Adam was slain, the Jew and the
Gentile—*as Jew and Gentile*—died, the one with

his ordinances and the other without, so that out of both might be created a new creation, neither Jew nor Gentile, but Christ. For only through the Cross and the slaying of the old Adam is the "New Man"—the Body of Christ—created; and there is no way into the membership of the Body but by way of the Cross. Then what he says about Jew and Gentile in Eph. 2, Paul declares in Gal. 3:28 about "bond and free" and "male" and "female." If the Cross slays the enmity between Jew and Gentile because both have died with Christ, it also slays the distinctions of "bond and free," "male and female," in the Body of Christ.

In the light of this sweeping away of earth's distinction between Jew and Gentile by the Cross, is it not clear that *the Cross has removed also the "middle wall of partition" between male and female in the service of God*? What difference is there between them before God, apart from the redemptive work of Christ? Has man or woman *any right within the veil except on the ground of the atoning blood*? Is it honoring the blood of Christ to believe that God bids a redeemed woman always enter His presence with a reminder of Eve's "fall" upon her head, or is she to point to the atoning blood and to the Cross of Calvary where the old creation life was slain and stand in God's presence under her new Federal Head—the Last Adam, the Lord from heaven? And stand also towards her fellow members of Christ's Body in the carrying out of the will of the Head in testimony and service for God. In the home sphere she is woman, wife, mother, sister, daughter, but in the Church and in service for God, praying or "proclaiming godliness," she is a "partaker of the divine nature," a messenger of the Lord of Hosts, a member of the heavenly Body, the Church—in both spheres seeking, with a meek and quiet spirit, to do the will of her Head in heaven.

As we consider all this, it appears that the spiritual understanding of the truth of the Body of Christ is alone sufficient to show that the words "Let your women keep silence" was the language of the Judaizers and not the "commandment of the Lord," for it is obvious that the Apostle would not speak at one moment of the "spiritual" status of the "Body," and each member as a channel of the Spirit and in the next moment lapse to the dealing with one section of it *on the status of the Fall!*

In the light of this truth of the Body of Christ and the need for its rapid maturing in view of the Lord's soon return, we earnestly pray that through this message every Christian woman who has been called of God to witness for Him in "proclaiming godliness" may be strengthened to fulfill her ministry, with the empowering assurance that the Word of God is in harmony with the call of

God which she has received. And we pray still more that the Holy Spirit may call out witnesses, male and female, to the Cross of Christ in this last hour of the Christian dispensation. That this was God's purpose for redeemed women, as well as redeemed men, was unmistakably expressed in the prophecy of Joel foretelling the outpouring of the Spirit at Pentecost. "Your sons and your *daughters* shall prophesy. . . . Upon the servants and upon the *handmaids* in those days will I pour out my Spirit," said Joel (2:28-29). He was one of the last of the prophets who could say, "Thus saith the Lord," before the "days of mingling" came upon the Jewish people, when there was no longer any prophet or vision of God. How the Holy Ghost came on the Day of Pentecost and how "daughters" and "handmaids" prophesied as they were filled with the Holy Ghost is recorded in the Acts of the Apostles.

And so it has been all down the centuries ever since. The Spirit of God has never been poured forth in any company, in any part of the world, in any nation, without the "handmaids" prophesying, and this as the spontaneous and unvarying result of the Spirit of God moving upon women as well as men, as at Pentecost. This invariable characteristic of all "revivals" is accumulative historical evidence to the mind of God on the matter, giving additional proof that 1 Cor. 14:34 and kindred passages should have been interpreted by translators and expositors *in the light of Acts 2* and not Gen. 3:16. For we dare not attribute satanic power, without danger of sinning against the Holy Ghost or quenching the Spirit in those whom God has moved to proclaim the Gospel, to every supernatural movement that has ever broken out in the church, or differentiate and say that only the men were inspired by the Holy Spirit and all the women at the same time, in the same place, were inspired by Satan. Counterfeits there have been in every movement of the Spirit throughout the ages working alongside the true, and counterfeits there are today. But there is one infallible test for distinguishing the false from the true—the testimony to the atoning work of the Cross of Christ.

We believe solemnly, as in the light of the Judgment Seat, that Dr. Bushnell speaks truth when she says, "The church which silences women will be found to silence the Holy Ghost," and "a sect, or sex, or race which attempts a monopoly of the Spirit's voice and power, will find that the Holy Spirit will flee far from it." We are in the throes of the most crucial changes in the world, when "our God is marching on" into the fulfillment of His purpose for the Church and for the world. "All things," said Paul, "are for your sakes." God's time has come for the emancipation of women, but it will be woe to the world and terrible loss to the Church if they are not won for Christ and for His service. For it is certain that if Christ does not get hold of the women of today, the devil will. And on the other hand, in the light of the Gen. 3:15 prophecy and evangel, it will be woe to the "serpent" and to his kingdom if those whom he has so oppressed and persecuted lay hold of the fact of his utter defeat at Calvary and in the power of their triumphant Head turn upon their foe in assurance of victory.

Let us pray for revival if the Lord still postpones His return and be ready to welcome all that is of God when the opened heavens are given.

May He set His seal to this message for His glory unto the ages of the ages. Amen.

OTHER BOOKS
YOU MAY WANT TO READ

THE FEMININE PRINCIPLE
by Judith Miles

A brilliant book which really gets to the heart of things. With unusual insight, Judith Miles explores such topics as beauty, fidelity, sexual fulfillment, liberation, love, oneness, pleasure, submission . . . and much more! This is the thinking person's *Total Woman*. $3.50

THE CREATIVE HOMEMAKER
by Mary La Grand Bouma

At a time when many are seriously doubting the relevance and workability of the family, a firm feminine voice is raised in defense of the age-old institution called marriage. Mrs. Bouma touches all the bases: being a wife, hospitality, child-raising, money matters, etc. She has written from a background of long, happy experience. $2.45

MOVE OVER, MOUNTAIN
by Nancy Life

The agonizing confessions of a middle-class housewife in search of peace of mind. Her attempts to find relief drove her to witchcraft, alcohol, and the brink of suicide before she finally began to experience the liberating power of God. $2.45

Purchase these books at your local bookstore. If your bookstore does not have them, you may order from Bethany Fellowship, Inc., 6820 Auto Club Road, Minneapolis, Minnesota 55438. Enclose payment with your order, plus 10¢ per book for postage.